My First Atlas

ALL ABOUT THE COUNTRIES OF THE WORLD

Written by
Kay Barnham and Robin Lawrie

Illustrated by
Robin Lawrie

Contents

All About Maps	2	C.I.S.	22
World Map	4	Africa	24
Around The World	6	The Middle East	26
The Changing World	8	Southern Asia	28
People of the World	10	Southeast Asia	30
U.S.A.	12	East Asia	32
Canada	14	Australia and New Zealand	34
Central America	15	Arctic	36
North America	16	Antarctica	37
South America	18	World Facts	38
Europe	20	Index	40

ALL ABOUT MAPS

A map is a picture of a place seen from far above.

A book of maps is called an atlas. It shows maps of every country in the world.

Watch for the mini-map of the world to see where each country belongs.

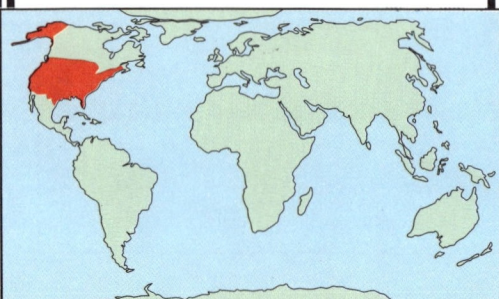

Maps can show places from near or far away.

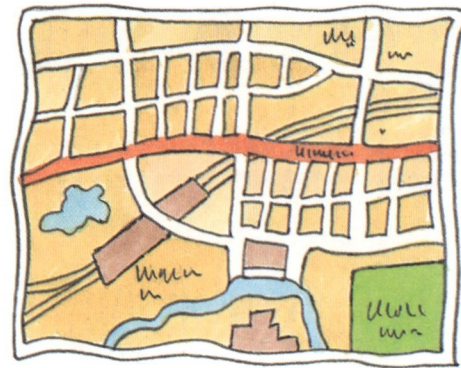

Some maps are so detailed that they show all the streets in a town or city.

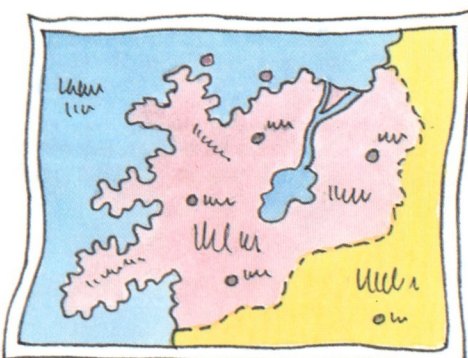

Maps of whole countries are shown from far away. Dots show where towns and cities are.

Maps cannot copy the real size of the places they show. They are drawn to a scale, which means that they are shrunk to fit the page.

MILES	250	500	1000
KILOMETRES	250	500	1000

A small distance on a map stands for a much larger distance in real life. The distance is shown under each map on a scale bar, which shows miles and kilometres.

The symbols below are used on the maps in this book.

Borders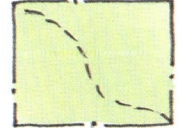

Capital cities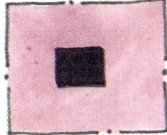

Large cities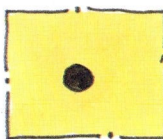

Lakes

Rivers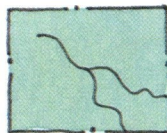

Oceans and seas

Mountains

Find out where different animals live in the world. Look for them on each map.

Explorers and travellers use maps to find their way.

You can use maps to see where you live in the world, or perhaps where you are going on holiday.

The index on page 40 has an alphabetical list of all the countries in the world. It tells you where to find each country in this atlas.

There is a compass beside every map in this book. This is to show you in which direction the map is facing.

North points to the top of the world and South points to the bottom of the world.

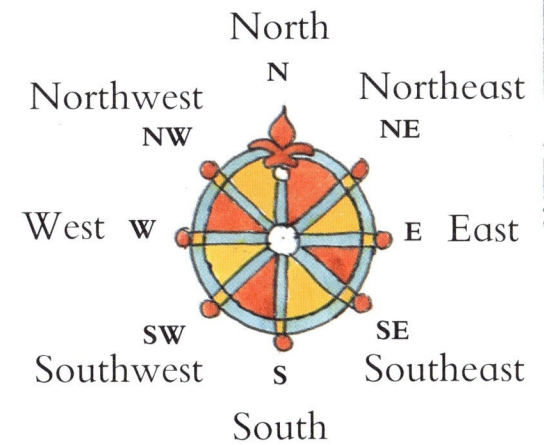

North
Northwest NE Northeast
NW
West W   E East
SW   SE
Southwest S Southeast
South

3

WORLD MAP

This is what the world would look like if it were flattened out. The seven coloured areas are called continents.

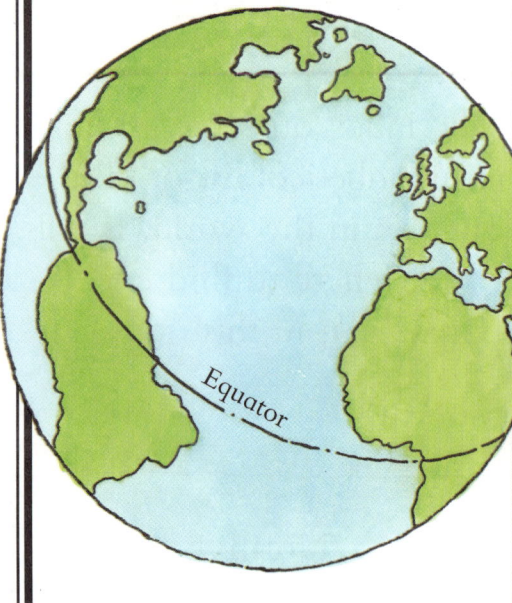

The Equator is an imaginary line running round the middle of the world, which divides it into northern and southern hemispheres. Europe is in the northern hemisphere.

North America stretches from the Arctic almost to the Equator.

Most of South America is below the Equator.

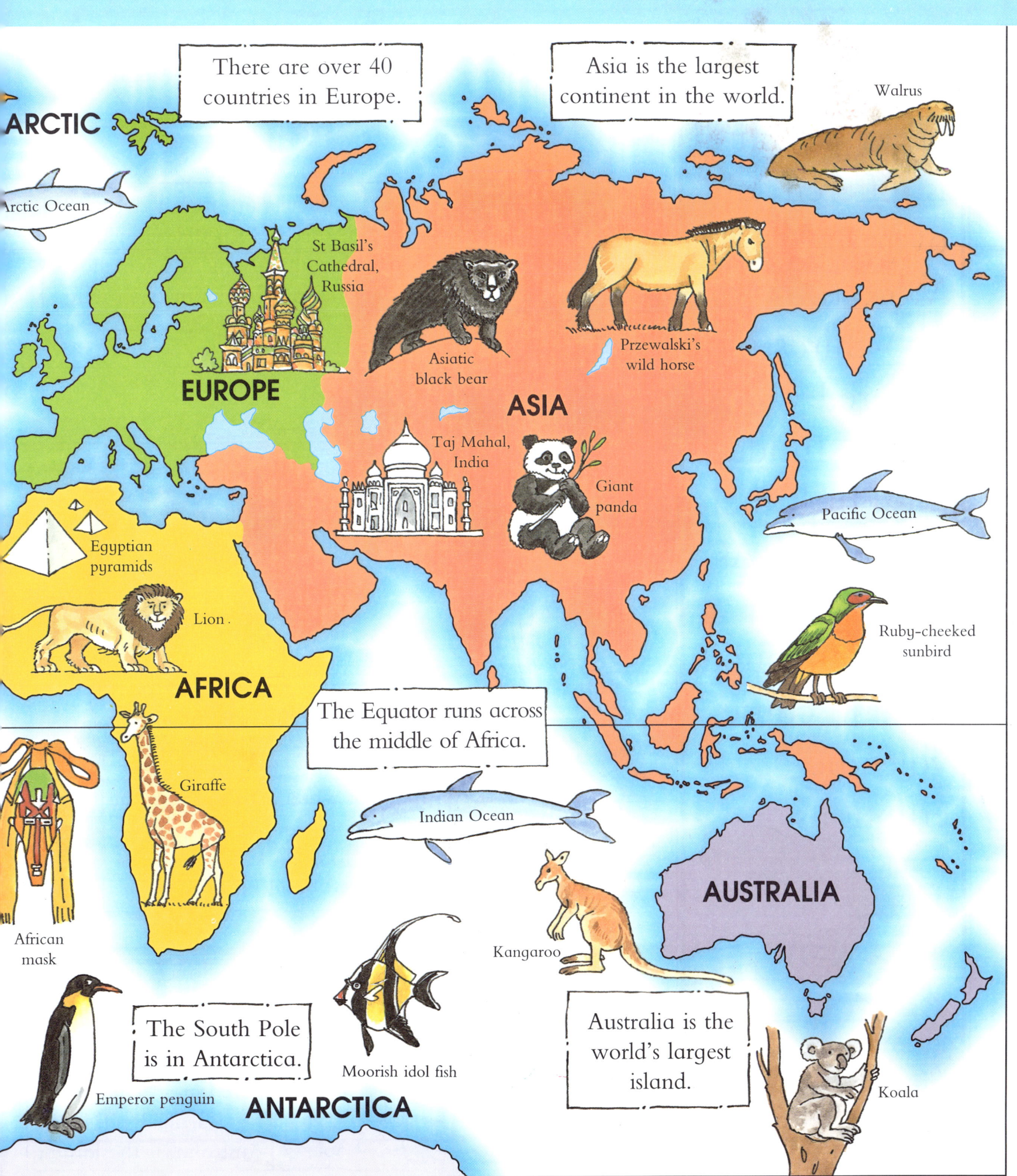

Around The World

The surface of the Earth is different all over the world. More than two-thirds is covered with water. Inside the Earth there are layers. As these move, heat can build up and cause volcanic eruptions.

Glaciers are frozen rivers of ice, which slide slowly downhill. Some glaciers move only a few centimetres a day.

Canyons are formed when rivers slowly wash the rock away. The Grand Canyon in the U.S.A. is more than a mile deep!

Geysers are hot springs that shoot hot water into the air. The most famous geyser is found in Yellowstone Park, U.S.A.. It is called "Old Faithful".

Coral reefs are formed in warm, shallow seas from the skeletons of millions of tiny sea creatures. The Great Barrier Reef, in Australia, is the largest.

The Changing World

The Earth was formed more than 4.5 billion years ago. Its surface was molten rock.

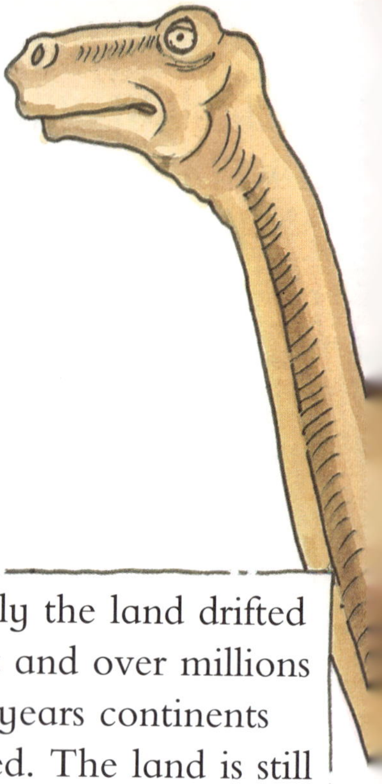

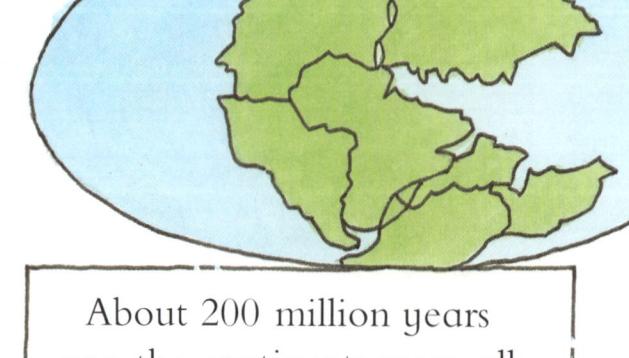

About 200 million years ago the continents were all joined together and surrounded by one vast ocean.

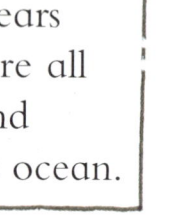

Slowly the land drifted apart and over millions of years continents formed. The land is still moving. In the future small seas will open up to become oceans.

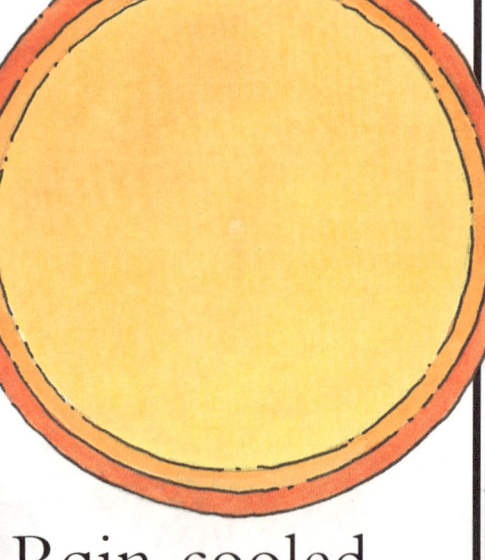

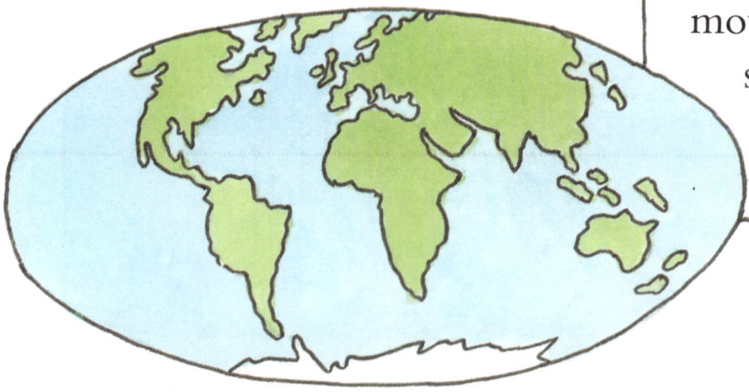

Rain cooled and hardened the Earth. The water formed shallow seas.

Large chunks of land, called plates, move by floating on a layer of hot, molten rock.

Fossils are the remains of animals or plants. They help us find out about living things from long ago.

PEOPLE OF THE WORLD

Here you can see traditional costumes that are still worn on special festival days around the world. Learn how people say "hello" in different languages, too.

There are over 3,000 languages. If you learn to speak different languages, you can speak to people all around the world.

France
"Bonjour" (French)

Italy
"Ciao" (Italian)

Denmark
"Halloj" (Danish)

Poland
"Dzien dobry" (Polish)

Greece
"Yia sas" (Greek)

India
"Namaste" (Hindi)

Some alphabets use different letters, and Chinese and Japanese alphabets have "picture writing" instead. There are over 65 different alphabets.

United States of America

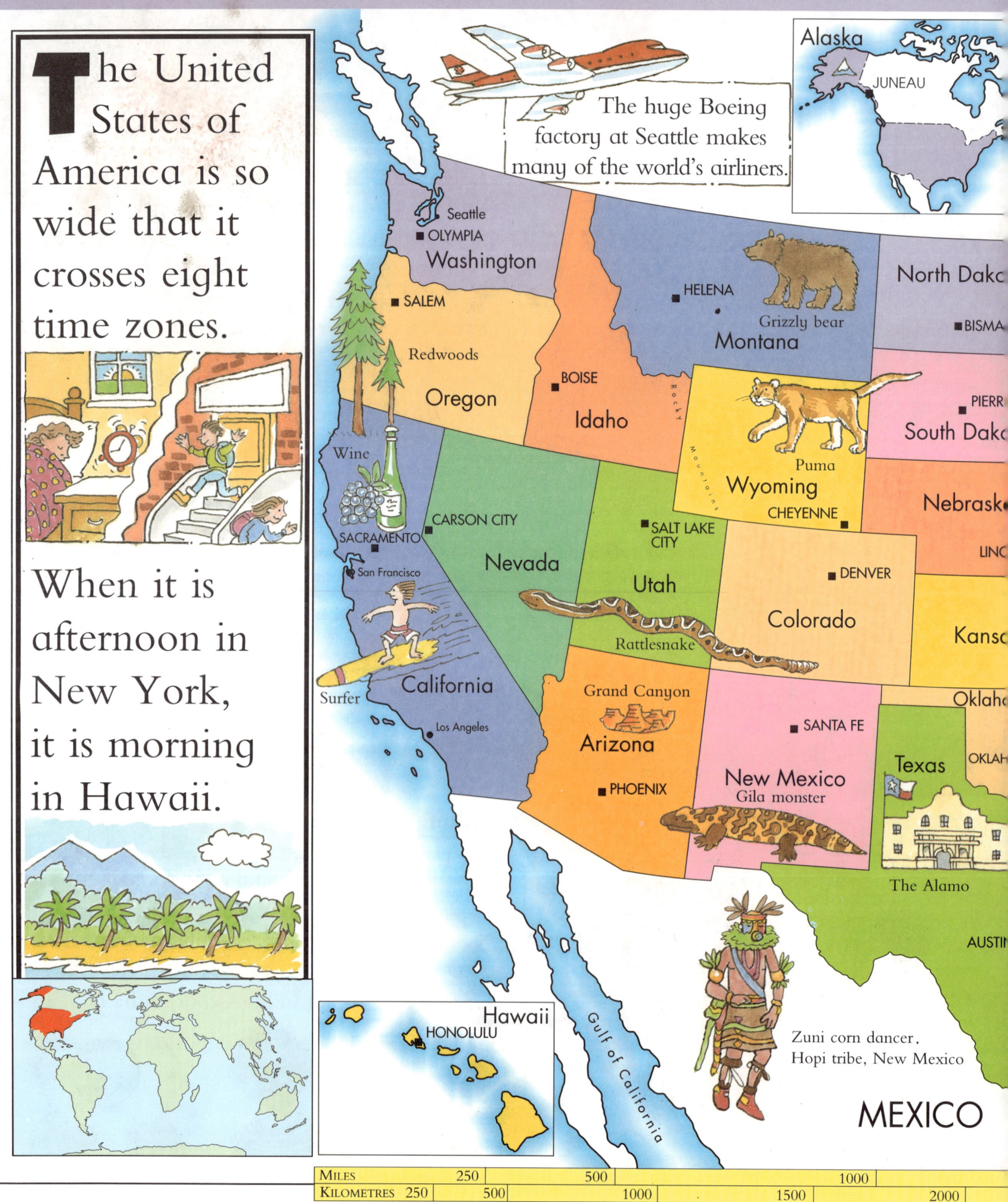

The United States of America is so wide that it crosses eight time zones.

When it is afternoon in New York, it is morning in Hawaii.

The huge Boeing factory at Seattle makes many of the world's airliners.

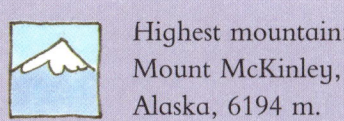

Highest mountain:
Mount McKinley, Alaska, 6194 m.

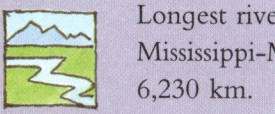

Longest river:
Mississippi-Missouri, 6,230 km.

Weather: U.S.A. is so big that the weather ranges from very hot to very cold.

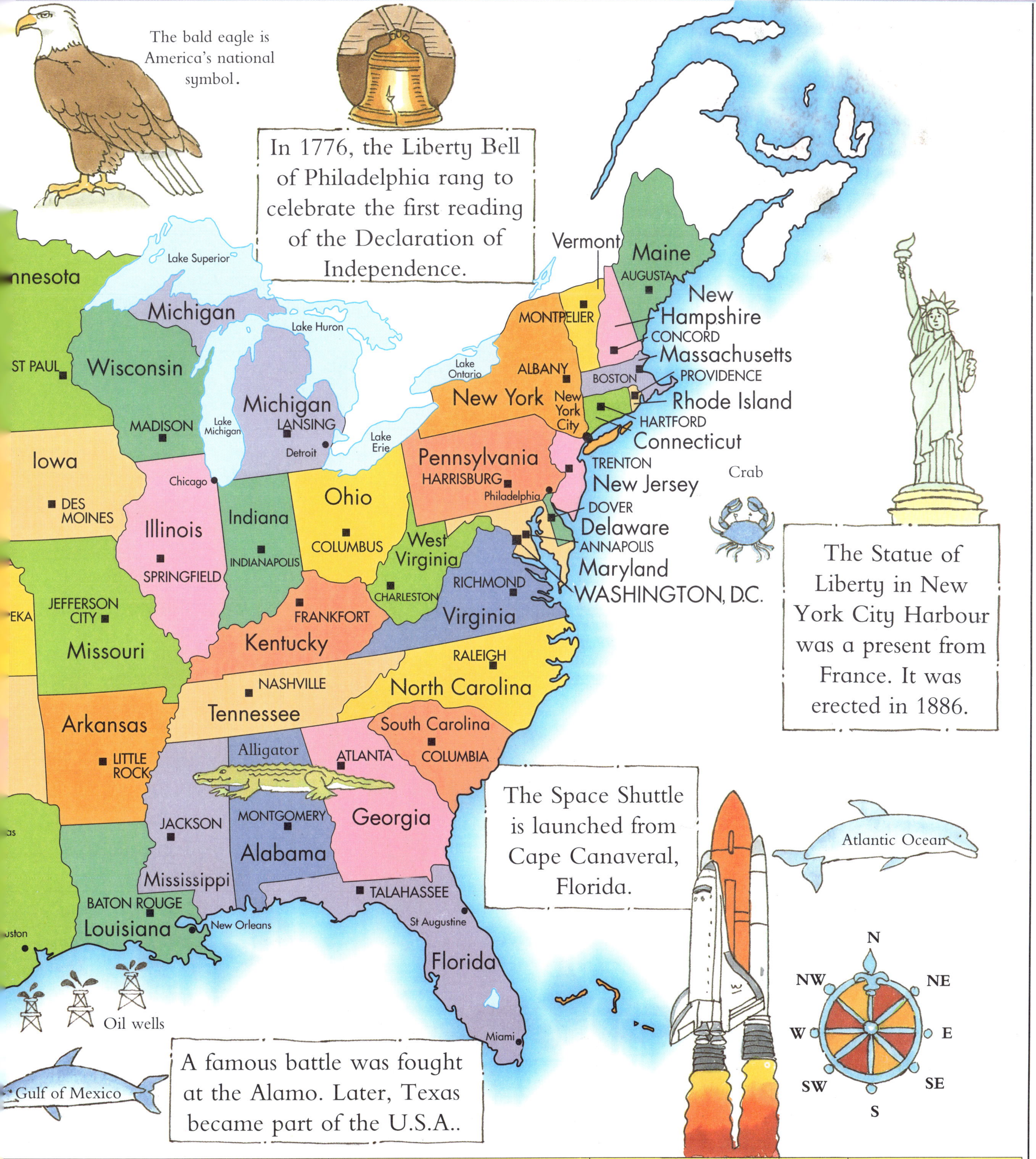

The bald eagle is America's national symbol.

In 1776, the Liberty Bell of Philadelphia rang to celebrate the first reading of the Declaration of Independence.

The Statue of Liberty in New York City Harbour was a present from France. It was erected in 1886.

The Space Shuttle is launched from Cape Canaveral, Florida.

A famous battle was fought at the Alamo. Later, Texas became part of the U.S.A..

1500 | 2000 | 2500 | 3000
2500 | 3000 | 3500 | 4000 | 4500 | 5000 | 5500

CANADA

 Highest mountain: Mount Logan 5,951 m.

 Longest river: Mackenzie 4,241 km.

Canada is the second largest country in the world, but has only one ninth of the population of the United States.

Most people prefer to live in the south, rather than the Arctic North.

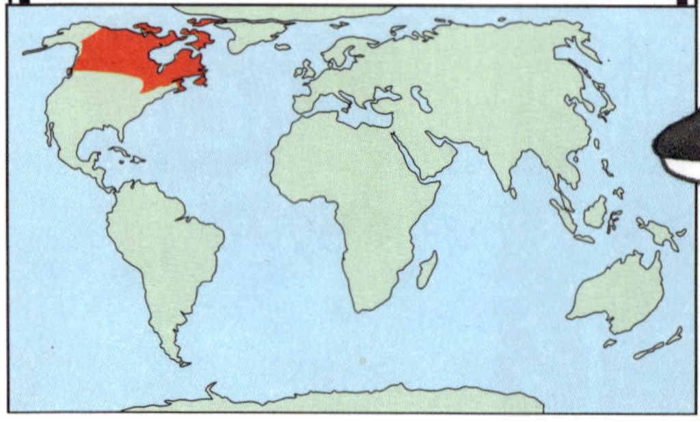

Mountain goat

GREENLAND

Arctic fox

Ice fishing

Mount Logan, YUKON, Mackenzie River, Great Bear Lake, WHITEHORSE, NORTHWEST TERRITORIES, Yellowknife, Great Slave Lake, Baffin Island, CANADA, Hudson Bay, Prince Rupert, Peace River, Lake Athabasca, BRITISH COLUMBIA, ALBERTA, EDMONTON, MANITOBA, SASKATCHEWAN, Lake Winnipeg, Vancouver, Calgary, Saskatoon, REGINA, ONTARIO, WINNIPEG, Goose Bay, NEWFOUNDLAND AND LABRADOR, NEWFOUNDLAND (ISLAND), ST. JOHN'S, PRINCE EDWARD ISLAND, Charlottetown, Fredericton, NOVA SCOTIA, NEW BRUNSWICK, Halifax, VICTORIA, Lake Superior, The Great Lakes, QUEBEC, Montreal, OTTAWA, TORONTO, Lake Michigan, Lake Huron, Lake Ontario, Lake Erie

Atlantic Ocean

Native American totem pole

The St. Lawrence Seaway links the Atlantic Ocean with the Great Lakes.

The Royal Canadian Mounted Police is Canada's national police force.

Canadian maple syrup is made from sap that drips from maple trees.

Killer whales are found along the Pacific Coast.

Ice hockey is very popular in Canada.

MILES	250	500		1000		1500		2000		2500		3000	
KILOMETRES			1000	1500	2000	2500	3000	3500	4000	4500	5000		

CENTRAL AMERICA

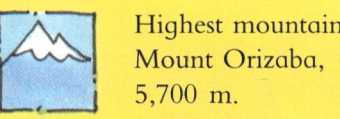
Highest mountain: Mount Orizaba, 5,700 m.

Mexico and Central America link the U.S.A. and South America.

Mexico is the largest country in this region. Much of the country is very high, dry and rocky.

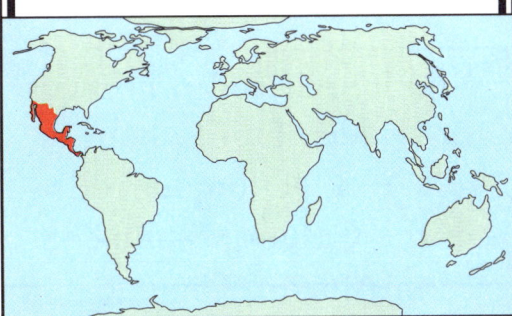

Spicy Mexican food, such as tacos and chili con carne, is popular all over the world.

More than 20 million people are crowded into Mexico City.

Jai alai is the world's fastest ball game.

Most of Mexico's oil comes from under the sea.

Aztec, Mayan and Toltec people once ruled Mexico. Some of their temples remain.

The Panama Canal connects the Atlantic and Pacific oceans. It can shorten a sea journey by thousands of miles.

MILES	250	500		1000		1500		2000	
KILOMETRES	500		1000	1500	2000	2500	3000		3500

North America

North America stretches from the Canadian Arctic down to Panama.

It includes the U.S.A., Canada, Mexico, and the countries of Central America.

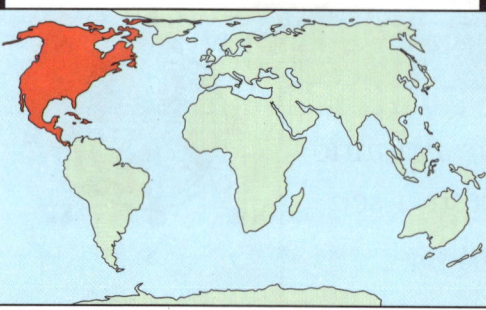

Plains (Sioux)

Southwest (Hopi)

Northwest coast (Chilkat)

Native Americans lived in North America for thousands of years before European settlers arrived.

One Californian giant sequoia tree is 84 metres tall and over 2,200 years old.

Oui! Yes!

Canada has two official languages — French and English.

The Pacific coast of North America is usually mild and wet in winter.

In Canada, snowshoes are used to walk on deep snow.

Wild horses, called broncos, are ridden by cowboys at rodeos. One famous rodeo is the Calgary Stampede in Alberta, Canada.

Miles	250	500	1000	1500	2000	2500	3000
Kilometres	500	1000	1500	2000	2500	3000	3500	4000	4500

SOUTH AMERICA

In the early 1500s, Spanish and Portuguese settlers arrived in South America. They conquered the native people.

Now a mix of Indians, Africans and Europeans live there.

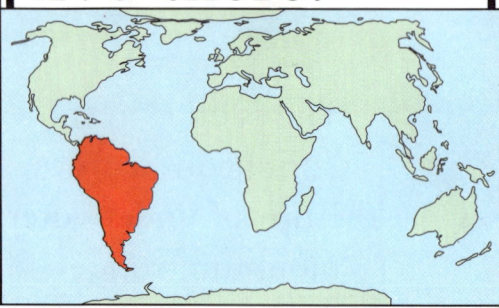

Giant tortoises live on the Galápagos Islands.

Rivers and streams feed into the mighty Amazon River from an area ten times as big as France. This area is called the Amazon basin and covers parts of Brazil, Peru and Colombia.

This area has more species of living things than anywhere else in the world. There are over 50,000 types of plants!

Farmers, lumberjacks and miners clear huge areas of rainforest every day. Without trees, the soil is soon washed away by heavy rain, leaving barren ground where nothing grows.

Andean cock-of-the-rock

Pacific Ocean

The Capybara, a relative of the guinea pig, is the world's largest rodent. It is over a metre long!

MILES	250	500	1000		1500		2000		2500
KILOMETRES	500	1000	1500	2000	2500	3000	3500	4000	

EUROPE

Europe is about the same size as the U.S.A., but has nearly three times as many people. There are many different cultures and more than 40 languages are spoken.

The Netherlands is known for growing beautiful tulips.

Atlantic Ocean

Historic Britain has many famous landmarks.

Switzerland was the first country in the world to produce chocolate bars.

Many famous painters lived in France. The country is well known for its wine and cheese.

Flamenco dancers

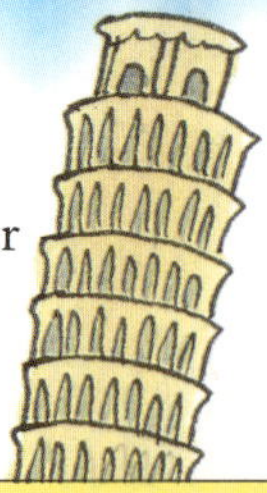

Highland dancing

REYKJAVIK
ICELAND

SCOTLAND
NORTHERN IRELAND
Belfast
EDINBURGH
DUBLIN
REP. OF IRELAND
Manchester
WALES
Birmingham
ENGLAND
LONDON
Thames

PARIS
Loire
FRANCE
Bordeaux

ANDORRA
Pyrenees
PORTUGAL
LISBON
MADRID
Barcelona
SPAIN
Ibiza
Menorca
Majorca
Gibraltar

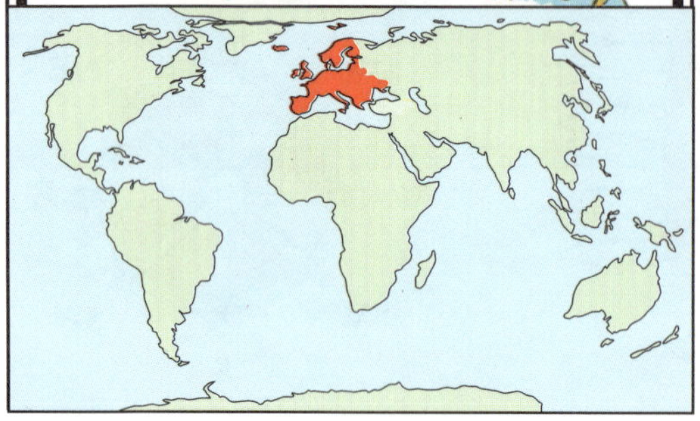

Leaning Tower of Pisa, Italy

MILES	250	500		1000	
KILOMETRES		500	1000	1500	2000

C.I.S.

C.I.S. stands for the Commonwealth of Independent States. It was formed from parts of the Union of Soviet Socialist Republics in 1991.

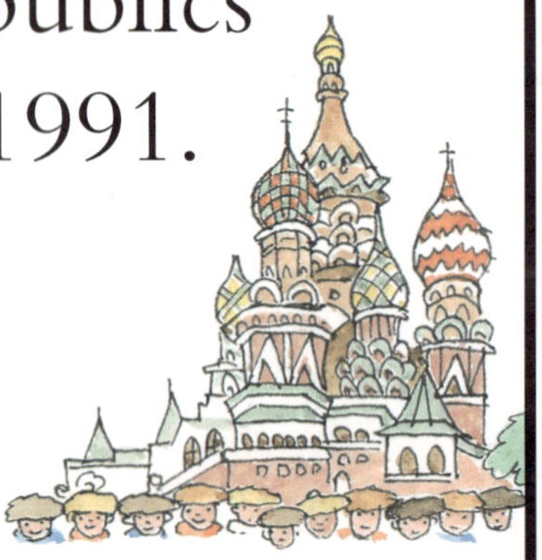

Russia is the biggest country in the world.

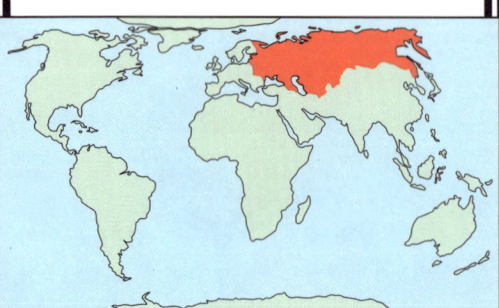

Moscow is the home of the famous Bolshoi Ballet dancers. They have performed all over the world.

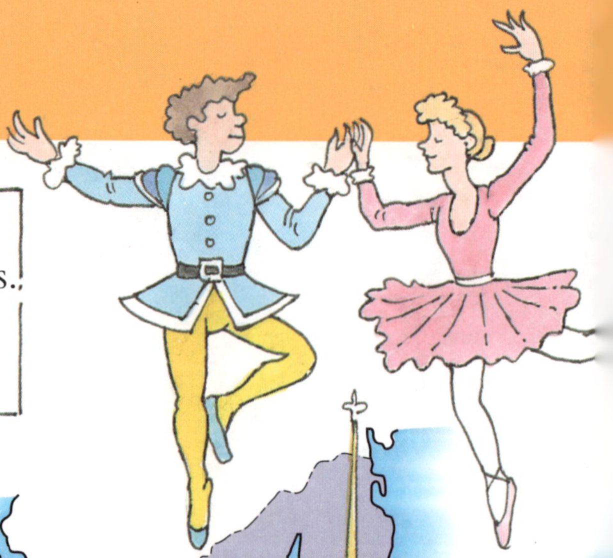

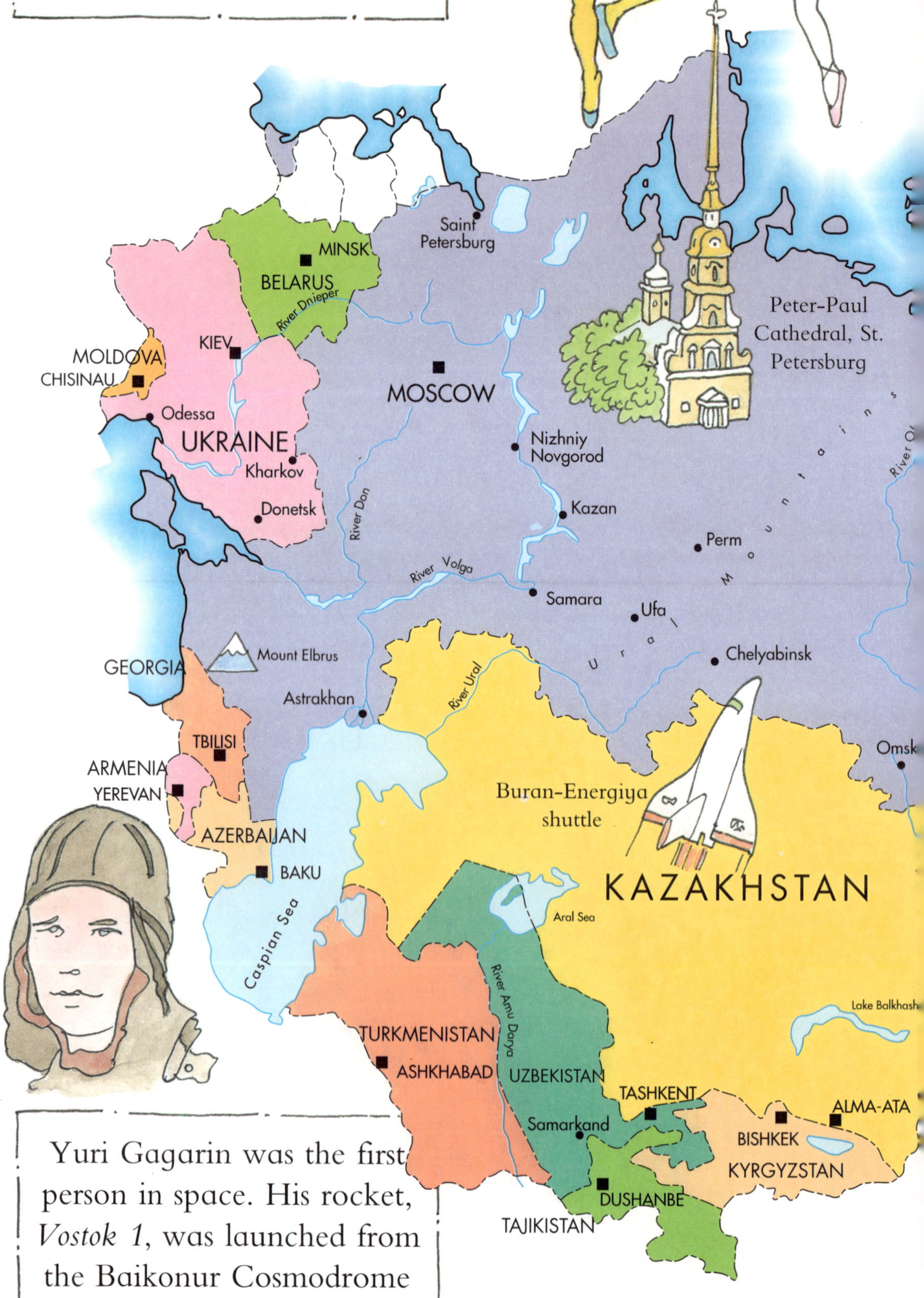

Yuri Gagarin was the first person in space. His rocket, *Vostok 1*, was launched from the Baikonur Cosmodrome in Kazakhstan.

MILES	250	500	1000		
KILOMETRES	500	1000	1500	2000	

| 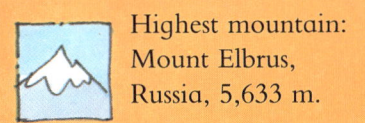 Highest mountain: Mount Elbrus, Russia, 5,633 m. | 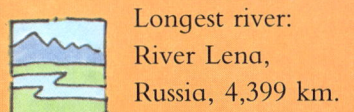 Longest river: River Lena, Russia, 4,399 km. | 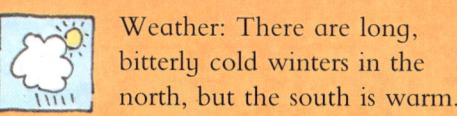 Weather: There are long, bitterly cold winters in the north, but the south is warm. |

The north is very cold in the winter months. Temperatures in Siberia can sometimes reach -60°C.

The Siberian coast is only 89 kilometres from mainland Alaska.

There are over 250 volcanoes on the Kamchatka Peninsula and nearby islands.

The Trans-Siberian Railway runs from Moscow to Vladivostok. It is the longest railway in the world!

Lake Baykal is the deepest lake in the world. One part is 1,940 metres deep!

Arctic Ocean · Severnaya Zemlya · Novaya Zemlya · New Siberian Isles · Asiatic black bear · RUSSIA · Cherskiy Mountains · Verkhoyansk Mountains · Kolyma Mountains · Tiger · Kamchatka Peninsula · Icebreaker · River Lena · River Yenisey · Russian troika · Sable · Sakhalin · Russian sturgeon · Novosibirsk · Krasnoyarsk · Lake Baykal · River Amur · Pacific Ocean · Altai Mountains · Vladivostok

N · NE · E · SE · S · SW · W · NW

23

AFRICA

There are about 670 million people in Africa - over twice the number of people in the United States.

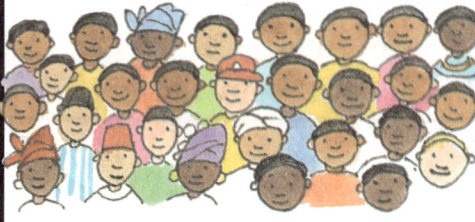

The world's largest desert is the Sahara Desert in Africa.

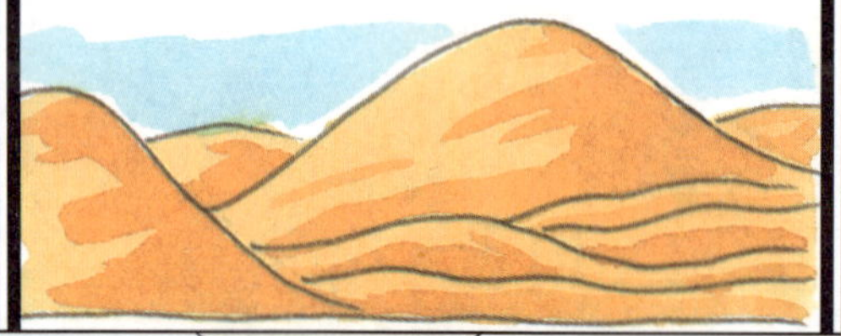

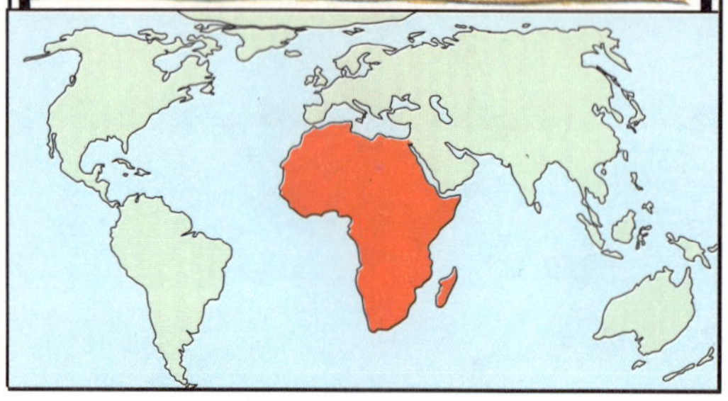

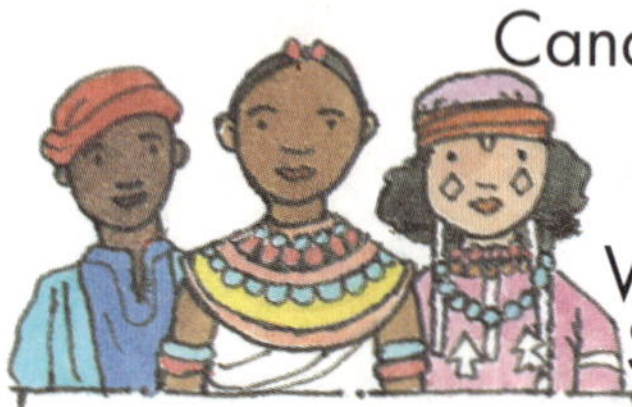

About 800 languages are spoken in Africa.

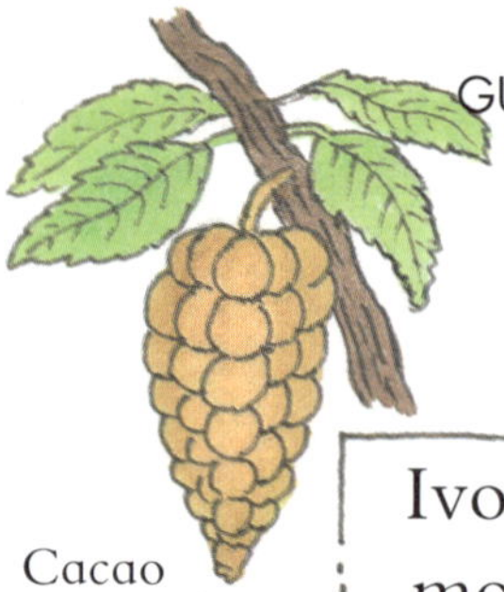

Cacao fruit

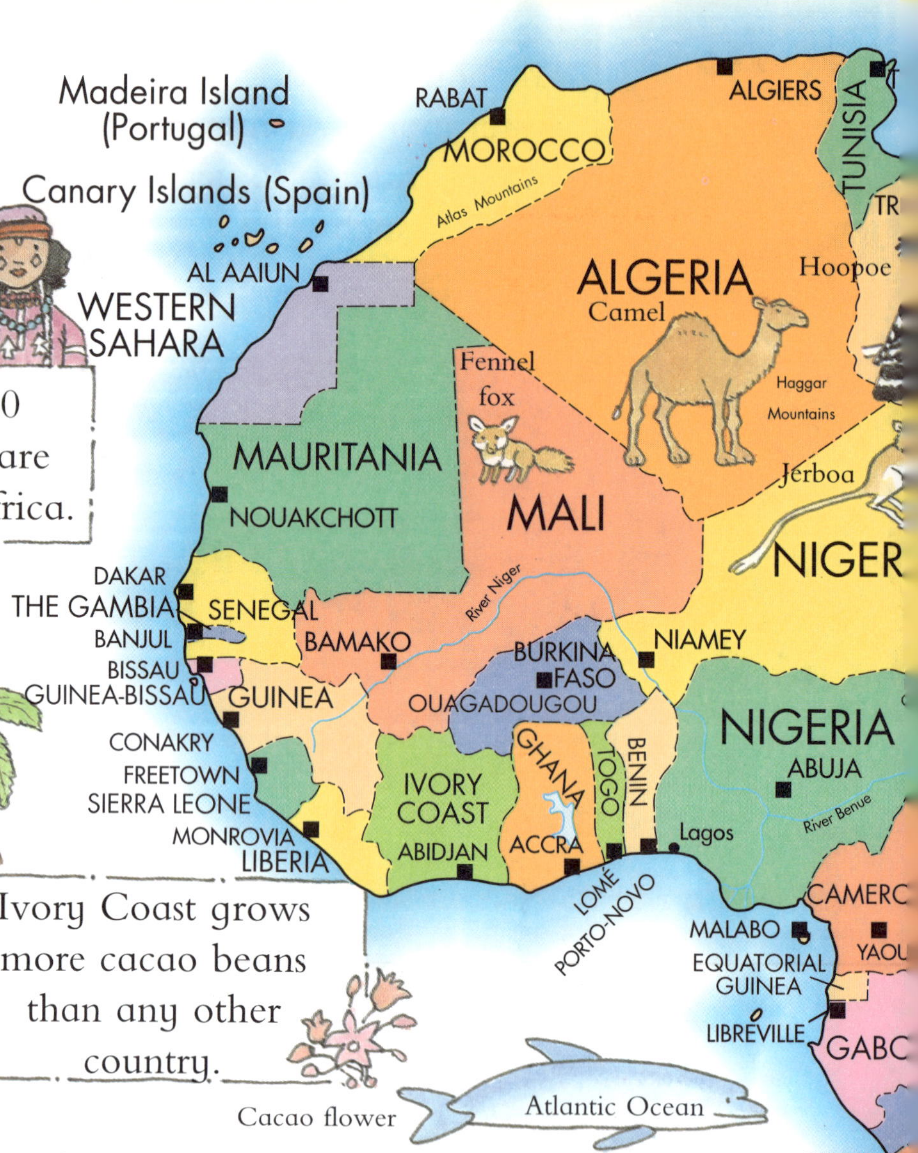

Ivory Coast grows more cacao beans than any other country.

Fruit, vegetables and crafts are sold in village markets.

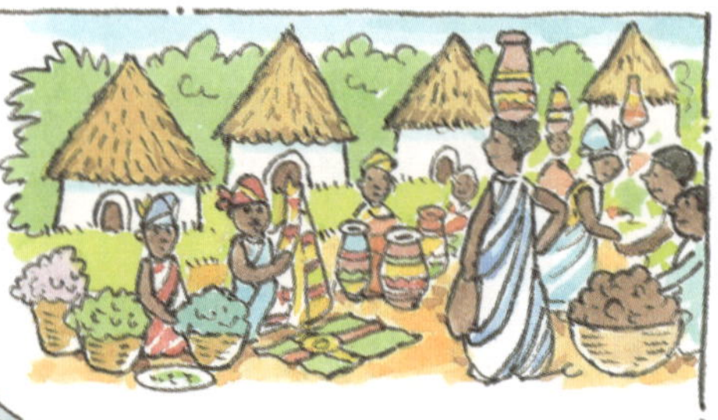

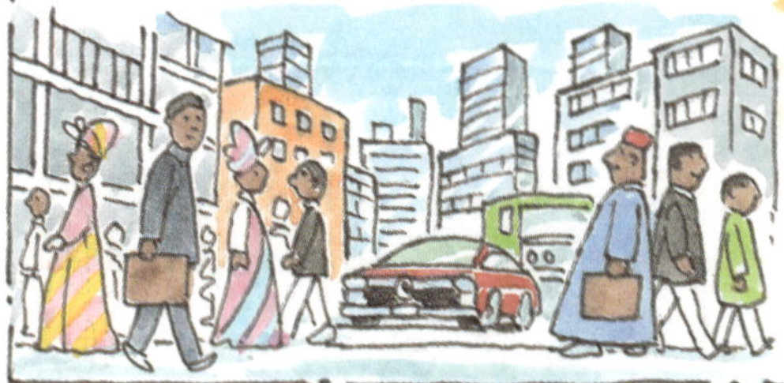

Many Africans are now leaving the villages to go and work in large cities.

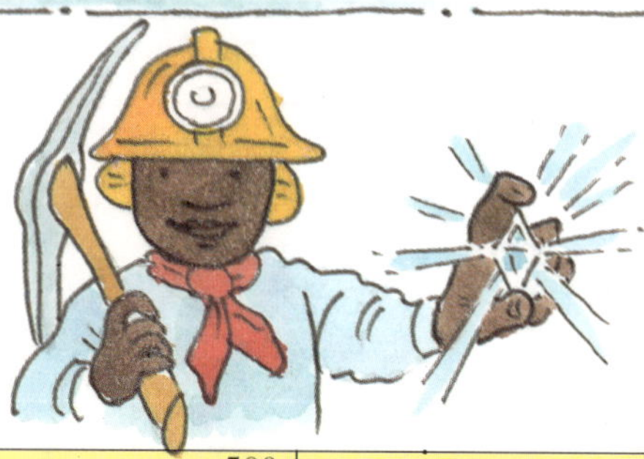

Diamonds are mined in South Africa.

MILES	250	500	1000	
KILOMETRES	500	1000	1500	2000

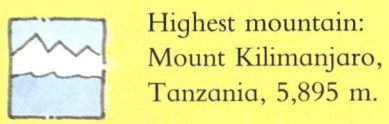 Highest mountain: Mount Kilimanjaro, Tanzania, 5,895 m.

 Longest river: River Nile, Egypt, 6,650 km.

 Weather: It is hot and humid at the Equator. The deserts in the north are very hot and dry.

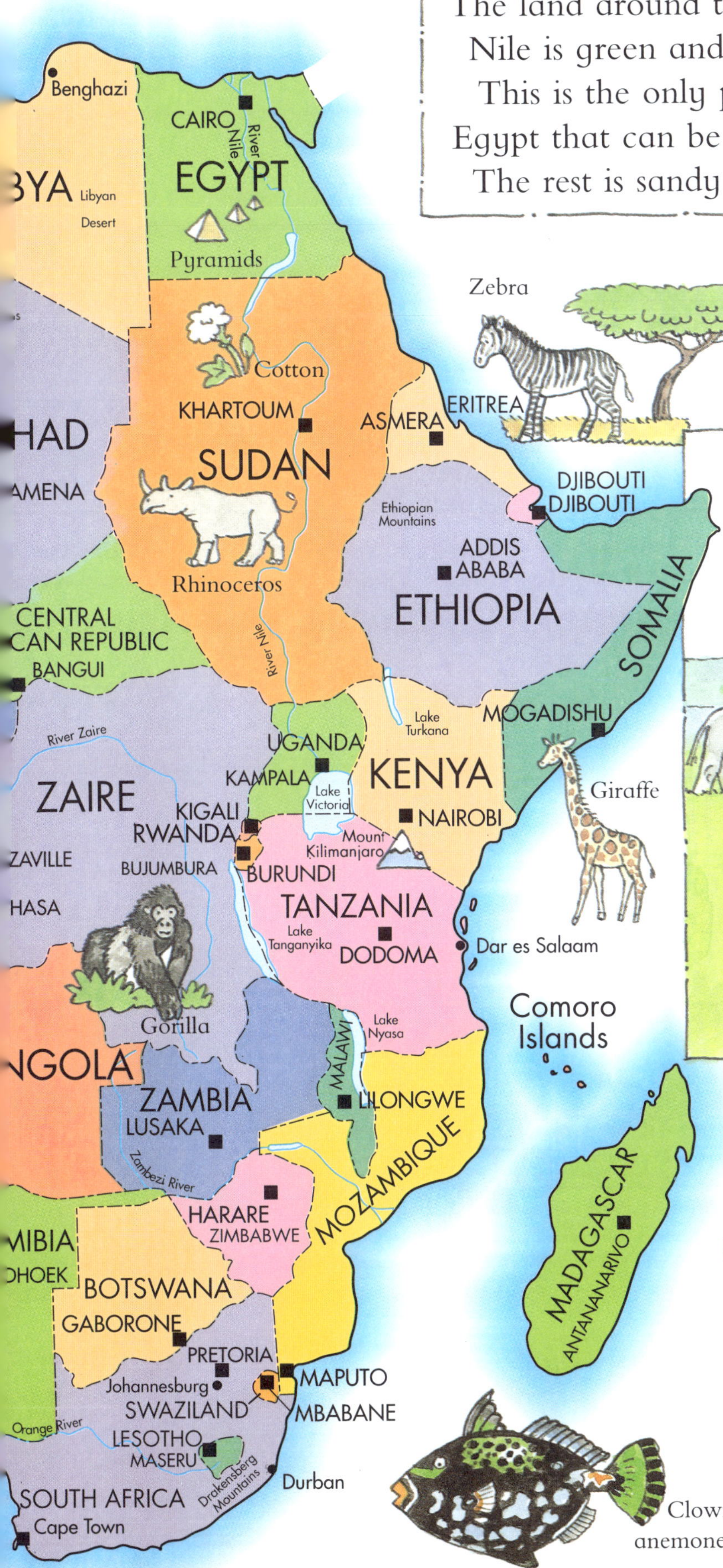

The land around the River Nile is green and fertile. This is the only part of Egypt that can be farmed. The rest is sandy desert.

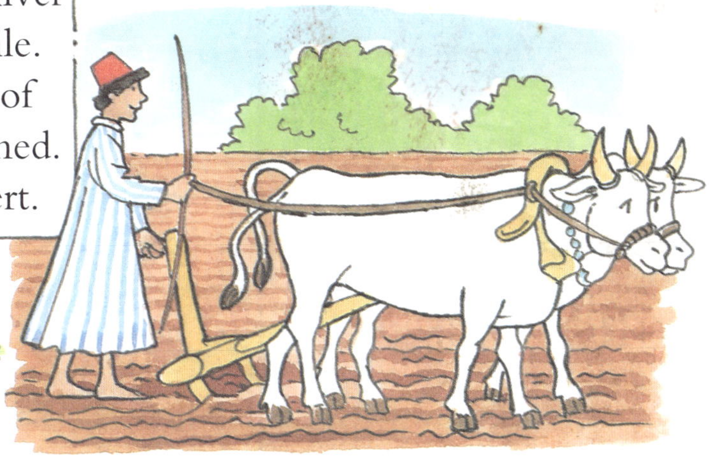

Africa still has herds of wild animals. They graze on the grasslands of the savannah.

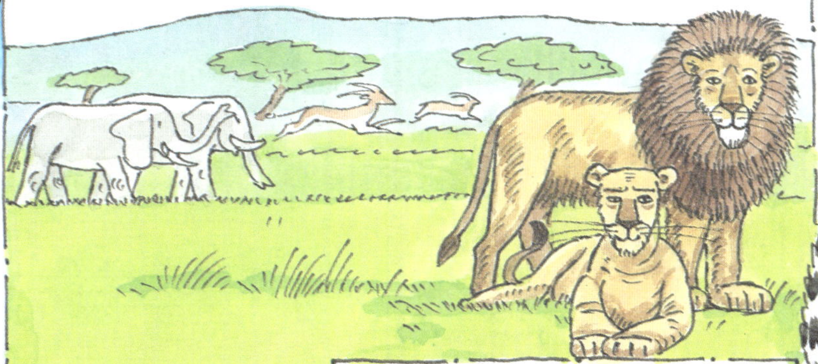

Many wild animals live in wildlife reserves to protect them.

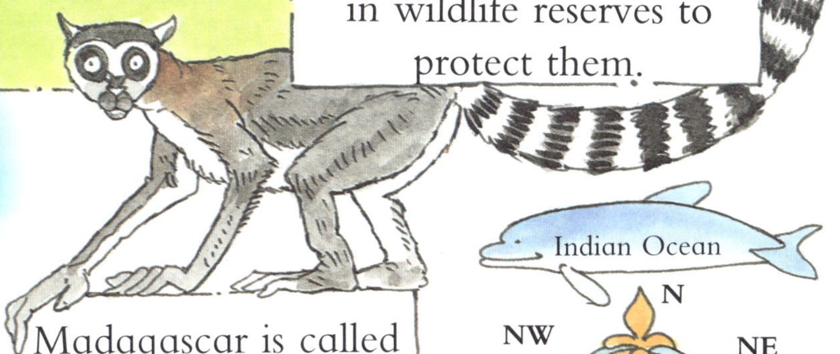

Madagascar is called the "Red Island" because of its red soil. It is the home of the lemur.

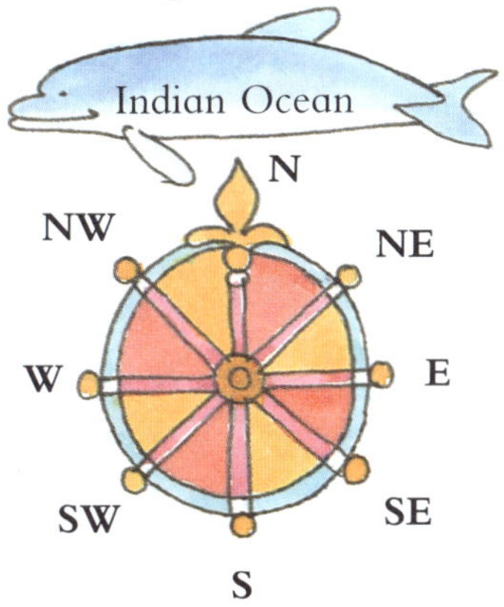

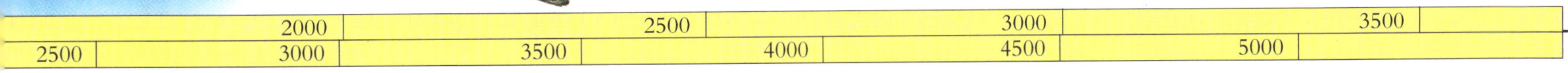

The Middle East

Most of the Middle East is covered with desert and mountains.

There is lots of valuable oil under the desert and seabed. Oil is sold to other countries to use as fuel.

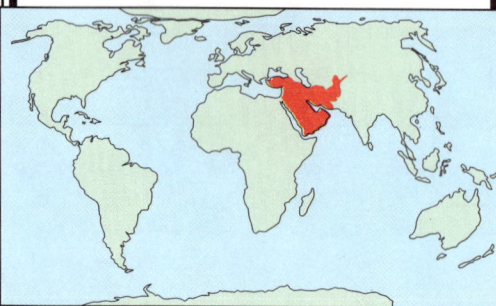

Black Sea

Istanbul

■ ANKARA

Taurus Mountains

TURKEY

Izmir

Marjoram

Olives

Melons

NICOSIA

CYPRUS

SYRIA

River Tigris

River Euphrates

LEBANON

BEIRUT

■ DAMASCUS

BAGHDAD

Mediterranean Sea

ISRAEL

Tel Aviv

JERUSALEM

■ AMMAN

IRAQ

Jerusalem in Israel is a holy city for Christians, Jews and Muslims.

JORDAN

Bedouin people

Dome of the Rock

Only Muslims visit the sacred city of Mecca in Saudi Arabia.

The Kabah

SAUDI ARABIA

A falconer

Jedda

Mecca

Hijaz

Arab "dhow"

Arabian Sea

The Rub al Khali desert in Saudi Arabia covers almost a quarter of the country. It is the largest stretch of sand in the world.

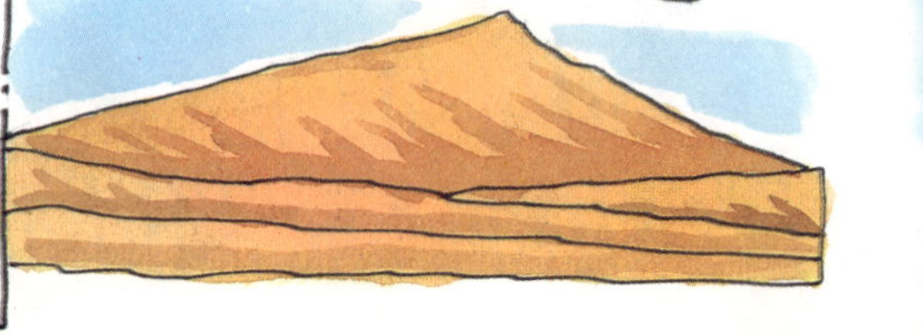

MILES	250	500		1000	
KILOMETRES		500	1000	1500	2000

26

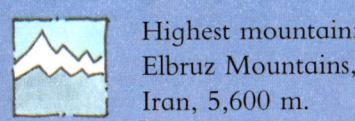 Highest mountain: Elbruz Mountains, Iran, 5,600 m.

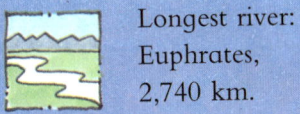 Longest river: Euphrates, 2,740 km.

 Weather: These countries have hot, dry summers, but in the north, the winters are often cold.

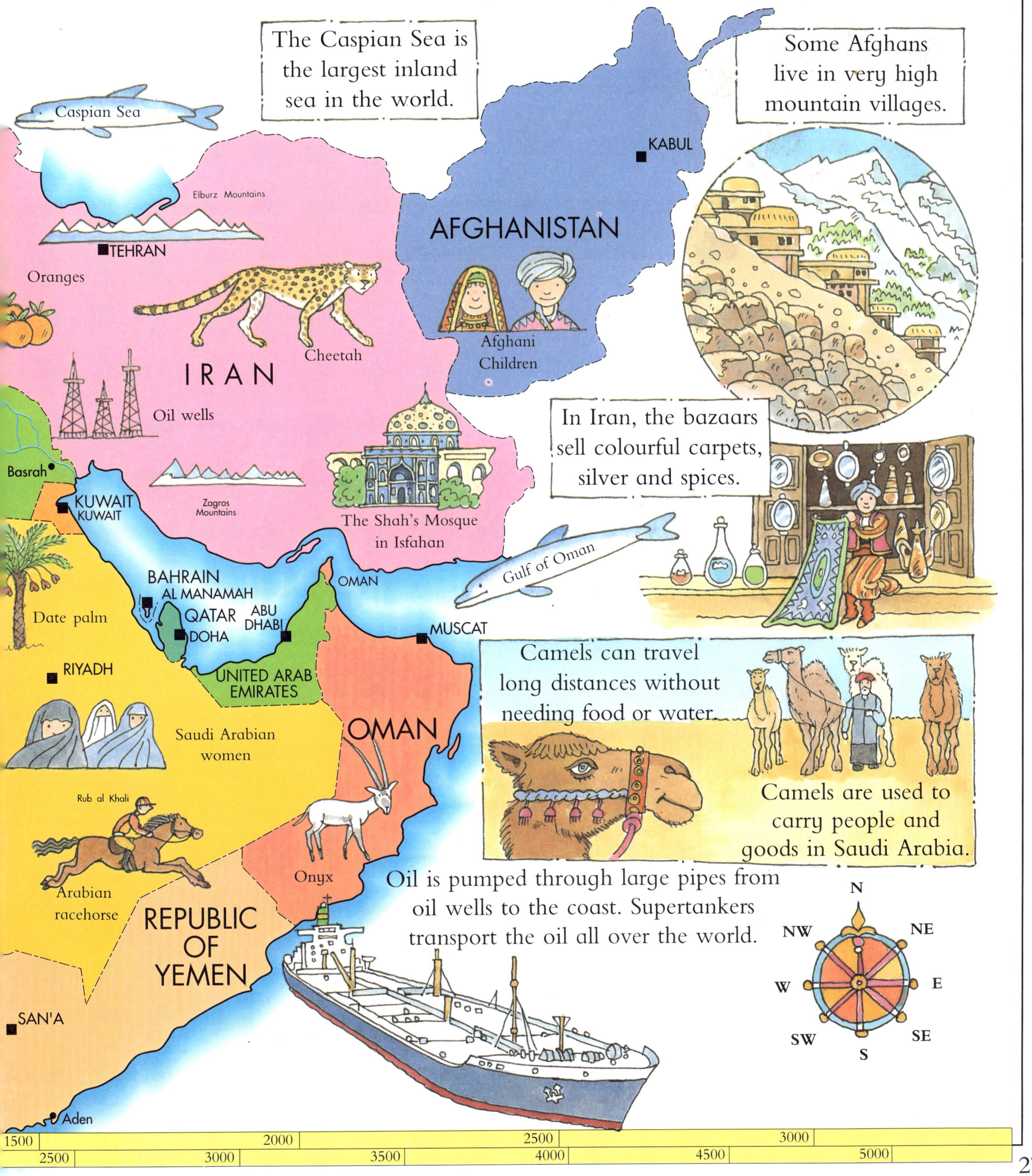

The Caspian Sea is the largest inland sea in the world.

Some Afghans live in very high mountain villages.

In Iran, the bazaars sell colourful carpets, silver and spices.

Camels can travel long distances without needing food or water.

Camels are used to carry people and goods in Saudi Arabia.

Oil is pumped through large pipes from oil wells to the coast. Supertankers transport the oil all over the world.

Southern Asia

Asian farmers rely on the important monsoon rains to make their crops grow.

If there is too much rain, floods can destroy crops and villages.

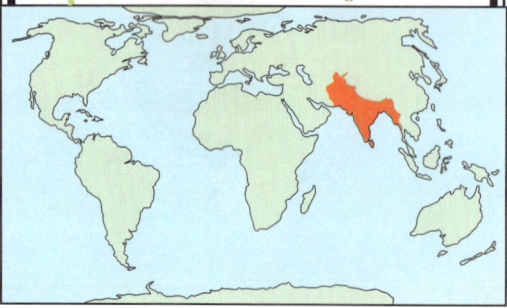

Rice Tea Coffee

One-fifth of Afghanistan's people are nomads. They wander from place to place.

KABUL
AFGHANISTAN
ISLAMABAD
Rawalpindi
Afghan "ghadi"
Lahore
River Indus
Blackbuck
Thar Desert
PAKISTAN
Indian elephant
Karachi
Ahmadabad
Bombay

Pakistan's official language is Urdu.

The Taj Mahal, near New Delhi in India, is made of marble. It was a tomb for an Indian emperor's wife.

More tea is grown in India than in any other country in the world.

Leaves from tea plants are picked, dried and crushed into tea leaves.

Miles		250		500			1000	
Kilometres	250		500		1000	1500		2000

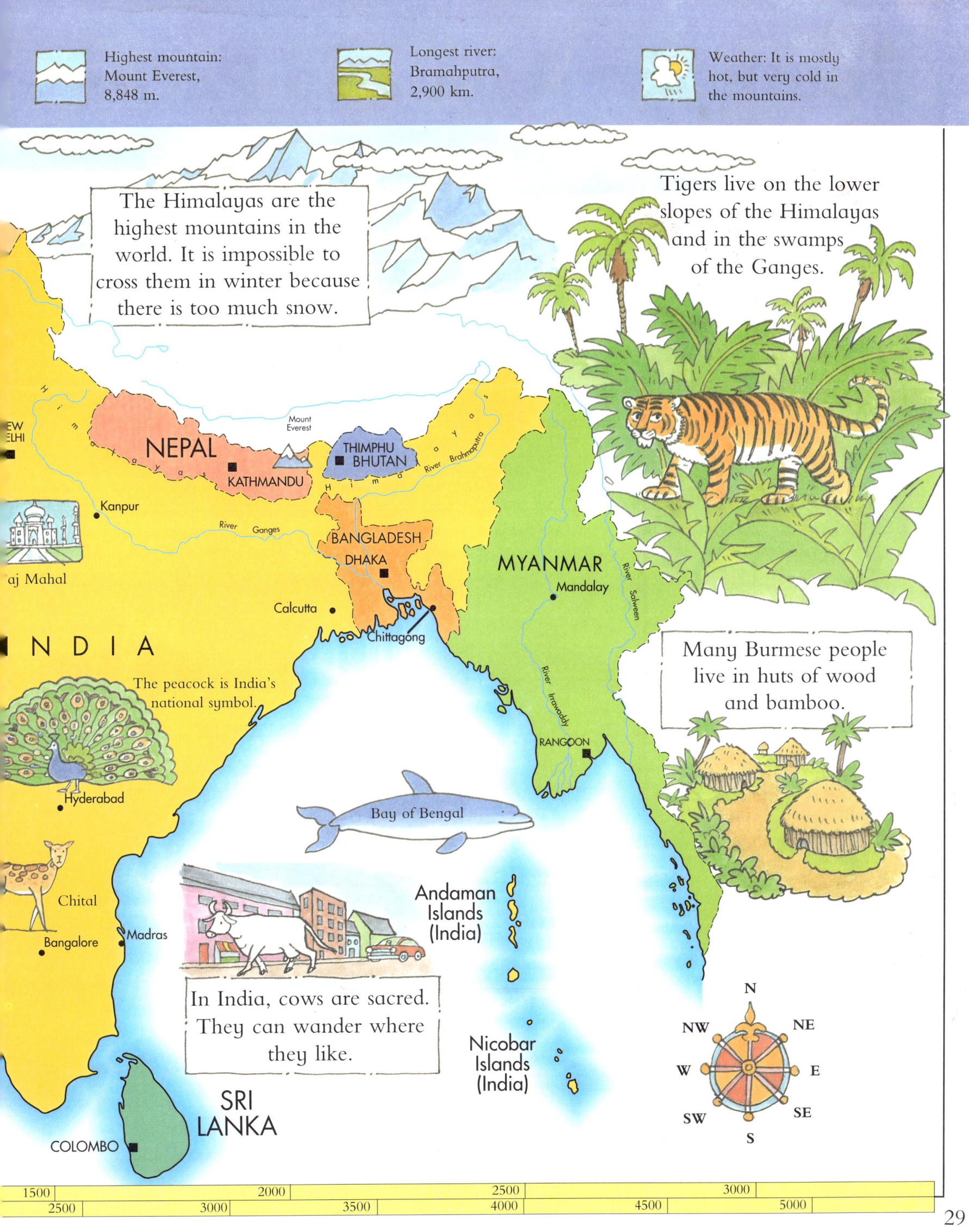

Southeast Asia and Pacific

The Pacific Islands curve from Southeast Asia towards Australia.

There are thousands of islands. Some are volcanic.

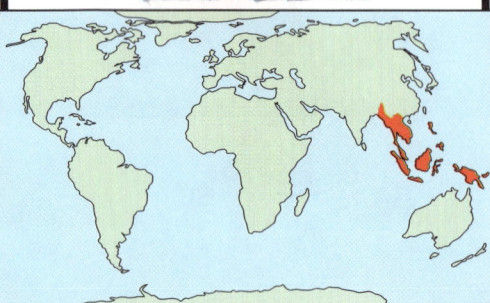

Tigers, rhinoceros, water buffalo and elephants are all found in Southeast Asia.

Many islands are made of coral. It takes millions of sea creatures' skeletons to form one small coral island.

Miles	250	500	1000	1500
Kilometres	500	1000	1500	2000	2500

ISLANDS

Highest mountain: Puncak Jaya, New Guinea, 5,030 m.

Longest river: Mekong River, 4,350 km.

Weather: It is warm all year, but the monsoon wind brings heavy rains.

Many islanders live by fishing. Their boats are like canoes with small sails.

Timber is floated down rivers from forests to the sawmills.

Farmers grow many crops such as rice, maize, tea, coffee and spices.

Luzon
MANILA
Pacific Ocean

There are hundreds of languages and many different religions in Southeast Asia.

PHILIPPINES

Mindanao
Davao

There are over 7,000 islands in the Philippines.

Celebes

Wooden house on stilts

Papua New Guinea is nearly twice the size of Britain.

ONESIA

Puncak Jaya
Golden bowerbird

PAPUA NEW GUINEA

PORT MORESBY

N NW NE W E SW SE S

31

East Asia

More people live in China than in any other country in the world.

Japan is made up of four large islands and thousands of small ones.

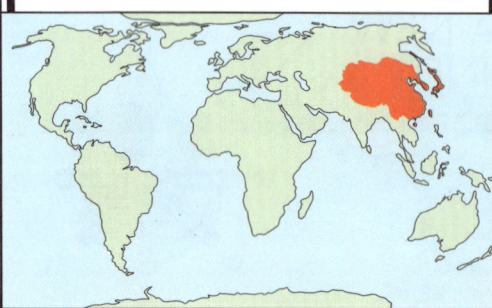

Mongolians are well known as expert horse riders.

The Great Wall of China was built to keep out enemies. It is 2,000 years old.

China's famous pottery and silk

CHINA

Yak

Tibetan Plateau

Mount Everest is on the border of China and Nepal.

Altai Mountains

Urumchi

River Brahmaputra

Lhasa

River Mekong

Himalayas

Mount Everest

China is the world's largest rice producer. The rice is planted in flooded fields known as paddies.

Miles		250		500			1000	
Kilometres	250		500		1000	1500		2000

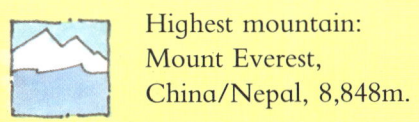 Highest mountain: Mount Everest, China/Nepal, 8,848m.

 Longest river: Chang Jiang, China, 5,530 km.

Weather: The north has wet summers and dry winters. The south is hot all year.

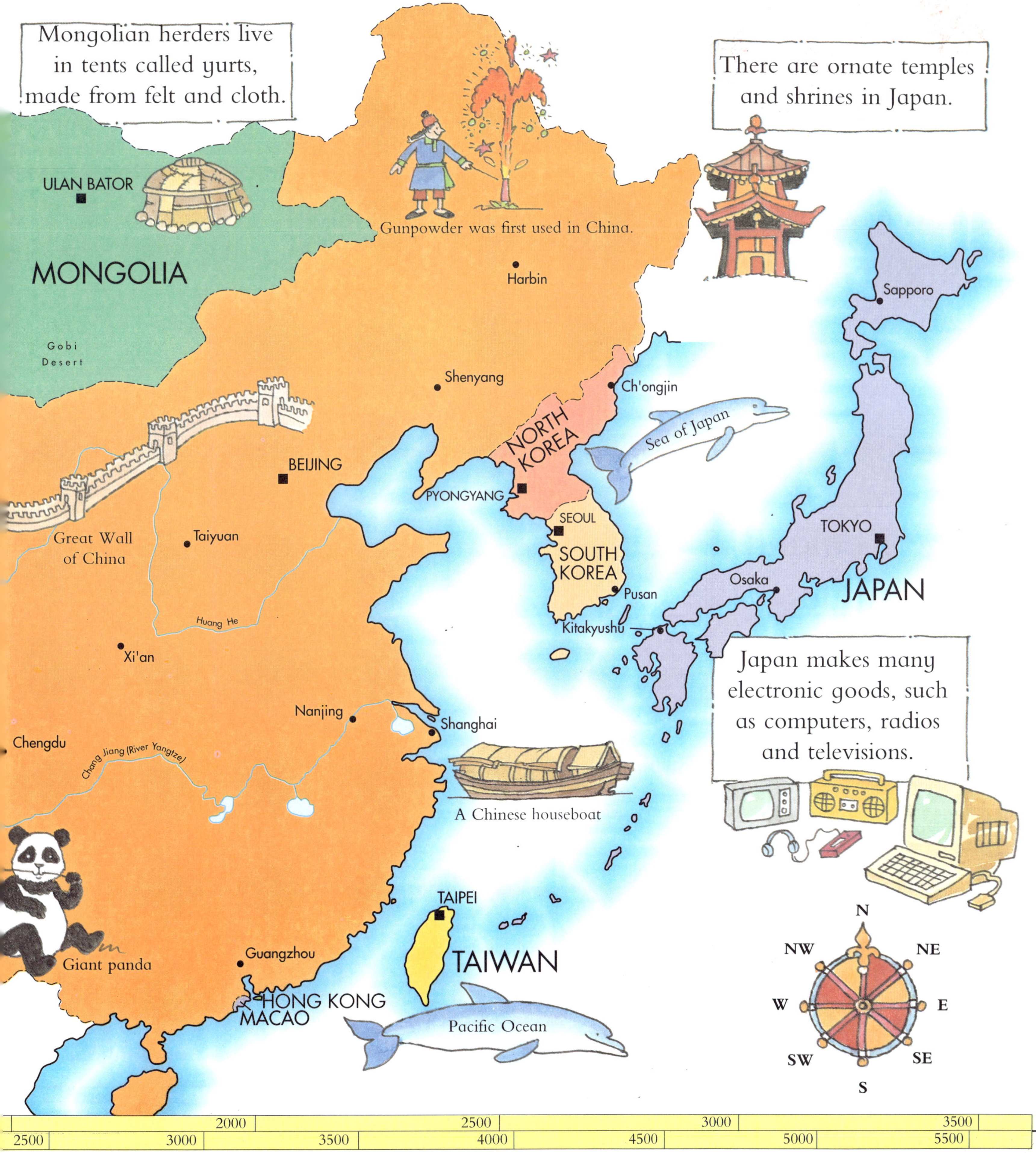

Mongolian herders live in tents called yurts, made from felt and cloth.

ULAN BATOR

MONGOLIA

Gobi Desert

Gunpowder was first used in China.

Harbin

There are ornate temples and shrines in Japan.

Sapporo

Shenyang

Ch'ongjin

NORTH KOREA

Sea of Japan

BEIJING

PYONGYANG

SEOUL

SOUTH KOREA

TOKYO

Great Wall of China

Taiyuan

Osaka

JAPAN

Pusan

Kitakyushu

Huang He

Xi'an

Japan makes many electronic goods, such as computers, radios and televisions.

Nanjing

Chengdu

Shanghai

Chang Jiang (River Yangtze)

A Chinese houseboat

TAIPEI

Giant panda

Guangzhou

TAIWAN

HONG KONG
MACAO

Pacific Ocean

N
NW   NE
W   E
SW   SE
S

33

AUSTRALIA AND NEW ZEALAND

A large part of Australia is very dry and barren. This is known as the "outback".

New Zealand is 950 miles southeast of Australia.

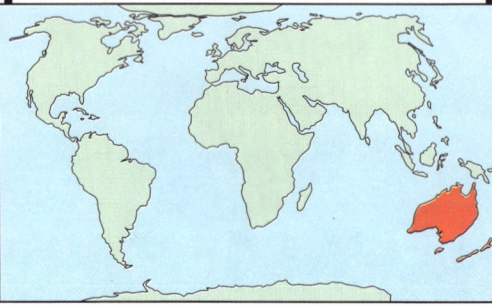

Australia has the world's largest wool industry. More sheep than people live here!

• Darwin

Kangaroo

A U S T R A L

Platypus

Hamersley Range

Emu

Macdonnel Ranges

Alice Springs

Giant Australian earthworm

Great Victoria Desert

1850s Gold Rush

Estuarine crocodile

• Perth

Indian Ocean

Aboriginal painting

Australia's native people are called Aboriginals. They were the country's only inhabitants until about 200 years ago.

MILES	250	500		1000	
KILOMETRES		500	1000	1500	2000

Arctic

The Arctic is the area around the North Pole at the very top of the world. The Arctic Ocean is icy cold and much of it is frozen solid for most of the year.

In 1909, an American called Robert Peary used dog sleds to become the first person to reach the North Pole.

The Canadian Inuits, who live in the Arctic, invented the kayak, a skin-covered canoe.

Lapps, from the European Arctic, use reindeer to pull their sleds.

Antarctica

Antarctica is at the bottom of the world. Unlike the frozen Arctic Ocean, Antarctica is actually ice-covered land. In some places the ice is 4,800 metres thick!

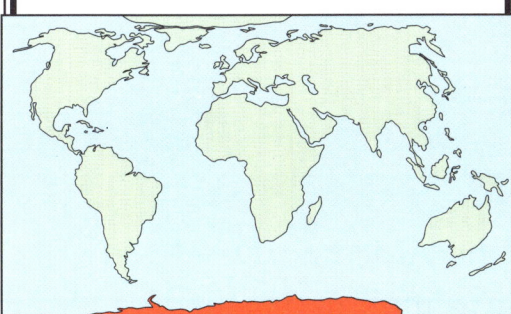

The ferocious leopard seal eats penguins.

Penguins can dive hundreds of feet under water.

In the future, icebergs may be towed to hot countries for fresh water.

Crabeater seal

Antarctic Peninsula

Weddell seal

Amery Ice Shelf

ANTARCTICA

Roald Amundsen reached the South Pole in 1911.

Ross Ice Shelf

Transantarctic Mountains

Pacific Ocean

Penguin

The skua eats penguin eggs.

Wilson's petrel

The only people who live in Antarctica are visiting explorers and scientists. It is far too cold for people to live there all the time.

Miles	250	500		1000		1500		2000		2500		3000	
Kilometres			1000	1500	2000	2500	3000	3500	4000	4500	5000

37

WORLD FACTS

COLDEST

Antarctica is the coldest place in the world. It can be as cold as -89°C.

OCEANS

More than seven-tenths of the world is covered by water. The largest ocean is the Pacific. It covers almost one-third of the Earth's surface - 166,240,900 sq km.

EARTHQUAKES

Some parts of the world have more earthquakes than others. They are near faults, where pieces of land rub against each other, making the ground tremble. San Francisco, U.S.A. is built near a fault and suffers from earthquakes.

SIZE OF CONTINENTS

Asia	43,565,000 sq km
Africa	30,262,000 sq km
North America	23,400,000 sq km
South America	17,806,000 sq km
Antarctica	14,000,000 sq km
Europe	10,521,000 sq km
Australia	7,686,000 sq km

WETTEST

Mawsynram, in India, is the wettest place in the world. Every year it has over 1,160 millimetres of rain.

DRIEST

In 1971, part of the Atacama Desert, in Peru, had its first rainfall in 400 years.

Deserts

The Sahara in North Africa is the largest desert in the world. It covers an area bigger than Australia!

Mountains

The highest mountain in the world is Mount Everest on the China/Nepal border. It is 8,848 metres high.

Largest Countries

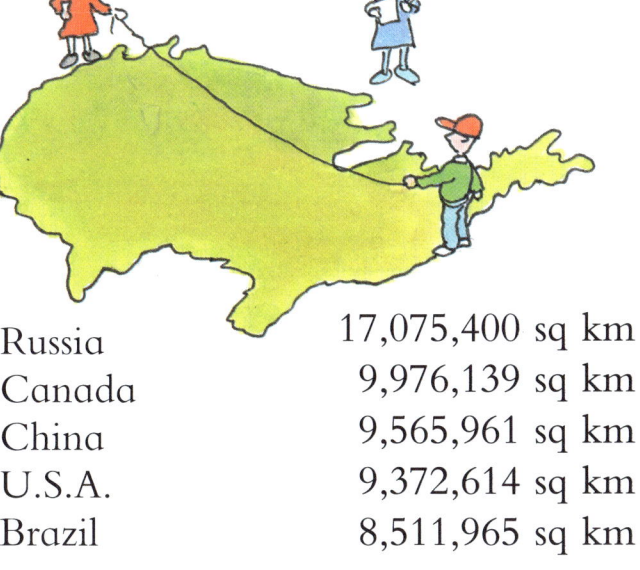

Russia	17,075,400 sq km
Canada	9,976,139 sq km
China	9,565,961 sq km
U.S.A.	9,372,614 sq km
Brazil	8,511,965 sq km

Hottest

One of the hottest places in the world is Death Valley in California, U.S.A.. Temperatures there can climb higher than 54°C.

Valleys

The Marianas Trench is a valley at the bottom of the Pacific Ocean. With a depth of 12,143 metres, it is the deepest valley in the world.

Volcanoes

There are 200 active volcanoes in Indonesia.

INDEX

A
Afghanistan 27, 28
Africa 5, 24-5
Albania 21
Algeria 24
Andorra 20
Angola 25
Antarctica 5, 37
Arctic 36
Argentina 19
Armenia 22
Asia 5, 28-33
Australia 5, 34-5
Austria 21
Azerbaijan 22

B
Bahamas 17
Bahrain 27
Bangladesh 29
Belarus 21, 22
Belgium 20
Belize 15, 17
Benin 24
Bermuda 17
Bhutan 29
Bolivia 19
Bosnia and Herzegovina 21
Botswana 25
Brazil 19
Brunei 30
Bulgaria 21
Burma 29, 30
Burundi 25
Burkina Faso 24

C
Cambodia 30
Cameroon 24
Canada 14, 17, 36
Central African Republic 25
Central America 15
Chad 25
Chile 19
China 32-3
C.I.S. 22-3
Colombia 19
Congo 24
Costa Rica 15, 17
Croatia 21
Cuba 17
Cyprus 26
Czech Republic 21

D
Denmark 21, 36
Djibouti 25

E
Ecuador 19
Egypt 25
El Salvador 15, 17
England 20
Equatorial Guinea 24
Estonia 21, 22
Ethiopia 25
Eritrea 25
Europe 5, 20-1

F
Falkland Islands 19
Finland 21, 36
France 20
French Guiana 19

G
Gabon 24
Gambia, The 24
Georgia 21, 22
Germany 21
Ghana 24
Greece 21
Greenland 36
Guatemala 15, 17
Guinea 24
Guinea-Bissau 24
Guyana 19

H
Honduras 15, 17
Hong Kong 33
Hungary 21

I
Iceland 36
India 28-9
Indonesia 30-1
Iran 27
Iraq 26-7
Ireland, Northern 20
Ireland, Republic of 20
Israel 26
Italy 21
Ivory Coast 24

J
Jamaica 17
Japan 33
Jordan 26

K
Kazakhstan 22
Kenya 25
Korea, North 33
Korea, South 33
Kuwait 27
Kyrgyzstan 22

L
Laos 30
Latvia 21, 22
Lebanon 26
Lesotho 25
Liberia 24
Libya 25
Liechtenstein 21
Lithuania 21, 22
Luxembourg 21

M
Macedonia 21
Madagascar 25
Malawi 25
Malaysia 30
Mali 24
Malta 21
Mauritania 24
Mexico 15, 17
Moldova 22
Mongolia 32-3
Morocco 24
Mozambique 25
Myanmar 29, 30

N
Namibia 25
Nepal 29
Netherlands 21
New Zealand 35
Nicaragua 15, 17
Niger 24
Nigeria 24
North America 4, 16-7
Norway 21, 36

O
Oman 27

P
Pakistan 28
Panama 15, 17, 19
Papua New Guinea 31
Paraguay 19
Peru 19
Philippines 30-1
Poland 21
Portugal 20

Q
Qatar 27

R
Romania 21
Russia 21, 22-3, 36
Rwanda 25

S
Saudi Arabia 26-7
Scotland 20
Senegal 24
Sierra Leone 24
Singapore 30
Slovak Republic 21
Slovenia 21
Somalia 25
South Africa 25
South America 4, 18-19
Spain 20
Sri Lanka 29
Sudan 25
Suriname 19
Swaziland 25
Sweden 21, 36
Switzerland 21
Syria 26

T
Taiwan 33
Tajikistan 22
Tanzania 25
Thailand 30
Togo 24
Tunisia 24
Turkey 21, 26
Turkmenistan 22

U
Uganda 25
Ukraine 21, 22
United Arab Emirates 27
United Kingdom 20
Uruguay 19
U.S.A. 12-3, 17
Uzbekistan 22

V
Venezuela 19
Vietnam 30

W
Wales 20
Western Sahara 24

Y
Yemen, Republic of 27
Yugoslavia 21

Z
Zaire 25
Zambia 25
Zimbabwe 25

This book was created by Blue Banana Books Ltd, The Barn, Randolph's Farm, Brighton Road, Hurstpierpoint, West Sussex, BN6 9EL

Editor: Kay Barnham
Managing Editor: Nicola Wright
Production: Zoë Fawcett
Cover design: Deborah Chadwick
Cover illustration: Peter Bull

Colour separations: RCS Graphics Ltd, Leeds, England
Printed by New Interlitho, Italy

This edition speacially produced for Bookmart Ltd

Copyright © 1994 Blue Banana Books Ltd
All rights reserved. No part of this publication may be reproduced, stored in a retrieval system or transmitted by any means, electronic, mechanical, photocopying or otherwise, without the prior permission of the publisher.

ISBN 1 85993
10 9 8 7 6 5 4 3 2 1